The Imitation of Christ for Children

The Imitation of Christ for Children

A GUIDE TO FOLLOWING JESUS

by Elizabeth Ficocelli

Illustrations by Chris Sabatino

Paulist Press

New York/Mahwah, N.J.

Cover and interior art by Chris Sabatino.

Cover design by Sharyn Banks
Book design by Lynn Else

Library of Congress Cataloging-in-Publication Data

Ficocelli, Elizabeth.
    The Imitation of Christ for children : a guide to following Jesus / by Elizabeth Ficocelli.
        p. cm.
    ISBN 0-8091-6733-6 (alk. paper)
    1. Imitatio Christi—Juvenile literature. 2. Spiritual life—Catholic Church—Juvenile literature. 3. Catholic children—Religious life—Juvenile literature. I. Title.
    BV4829.F45 2006
    248.8′2—dc22

                                                        2006006623

Published by Paulist Press
997 Macarthur Boulevard
Mahwah, New Jersey 07430

www.paulistpress.com

Printed and bound in the
United States of America

Contents

For Susan Heyboer O'Keefe
Editor, mentor, friend
E. F.

Introduction
A Very Special Book

This book is based on a very special book written over five hundred years ago called *The Imitation of Christ*. The original book was written by a man named Thomas à Kempis, which means "Thomas of Kempen," the town in Germany where he was born, somewhere around the year 1380.

The Imitation of Christ has been a favorite for millions of people around the world because it contains rich treasure. This is not the kind of treasure that pirates scoured the oceans for, or that kings locked away in stony castles. It is the kind of treasure Jesus spoke about in the Bible when he said:

> *"Do not store up for yourselves treasures on earth, where moth and rust consume and where thieves break in and steal, but store up for yourselves treasures in heaven, where neither moth nor rust consumes and where thieves do not break in and steal. For where your treasure is, there your heart will be also."*
>
> *(Matthew 6:19–21)*

The treasure Jesus is speaking about is far more valuable than jewels or coins or pieces of art because it refers to things that are lasting: faith in God, love of neighbor, peace of heart,

1

heavenly wisdom, and truth. These are things that bring people true joy and satisfaction. These are things that do not pass away with time.

Thomas à Kempis

Since Thomas lived such a long time ago, we don't know much about his life. We do know that when he was only thirteen years old, he left his home in Germany and set out after his older brother, John, to attend school in the nearby country of the Netherlands, or Holland. Thomas arrived in the Netherlands to learn that his brother was a member of a new religious order that he had helped to form, called the *Brothers of the Common Life*. Thomas was curious and wanted to know more.

He found his brother living in a community similar to that of the early Christians. This group of holy men earned their living with their own hands and shared their food, money, and what little they owned. Their life was simple, focused on prayer, work, and the love of God and neighbor. Thomas was very impressed by the faith of these men, and his heart felt called to join them. When he presented himself to the community, the brothers received him warmly as a student.

In those days, there were no computers or typewriters or printing presses. Books, including the Bible, were copied by hand, letter by letter, with pen and ink. This was one of the most important ways the brothers earned their living. Thomas showed an immediate gift for copying manuscripts neatly and accurately. As a result, he spent much of his life performing this task. He loved books, particularly the Bible, and the long hours he spent copying it allowed the wisdom and beauty of the passages to sink deep into his soul.

The Purpose of Life

Thomas's reading and copying made him a strong student and a devout brother, as his love for God deepened. Through years of study and prayer, Thomas came to a great realization: the only purpose in life is to praise, love, and serve God. He saw how people liked to make things very complicated, how they liked to put themselves in control of everything to the point where they thought they did not need God at all. But Thomas knew this was a big mistake. He understood that all of us are completely dependent on God—*we simply cannot exist without him.*

Thomas also understood that the best way to love and serve God is to follow the example set by his Son, Jesus, in his teachings, his life, and his passion and death. Thomas tried hard to follow in Jesus' footsteps. He listened to Jesus' words and applied them to his own life. Thomas was known to be kind to all, particularly those who suffered. He avoided gossip and idle conversation, except when the subject turned to God. Thomas willingly made sacrifices, bore his difficulties with patience, and worked constantly to change things about himself to be a better disciple of Jesus.

In time, Thomas began to write books of his own, explaining some of his thoughts and ideas. The most famous book he wrote was *The Imitation of Christ*. By this time, Thomas was an ordained priest, and he was in charge of the spiritual development of the brothers. Thomas wanted to help the men in his community come to know and love God as he did. He wanted them to be as close to God as possible. So he wrote a book of instruction, using simple terms, loving words, and practical ideas. The brothers were greatly helped by this book. Soon, the book became so popular that it was shared outside the community, first with other religious orders and then with the public. Thomas's teachings were so beautiful, honest, and logical that everyone wanted to read them.

But Life Is Different Today!

It's true: the world of Thomas à Kempis was different from our own. It had its own set of problems and pressures. Today, kids are faced with some pretty tough issues, much harder issues than their parents or grandparents ever had to deal with. On top of the usual stuff like being accepted by other kids, getting good grades, feeling good about themselves, and figuring out what they want to be when they grow up, kids today have to deal with drugs, alcohol, divorce, teen pregnancy, depression, child abuse, and violence—just to name a few. Sometimes, it's really hard to be a kid. It seems there's so much pressure to grow up.

The good news is that growing up doesn't have to be so difficult. Each of us, no matter how alone or misunderstood we may feel from time to time, has someone who understands us and cares about us. That person is Jesus, the same Jesus who walked the earth two thousand years ago, the same Jesus whom Thomas à Kempis grew to know and love, and the same Jesus who watches over us today and tomorrow. He knows everything about us, and he knew it even before we were born!

You Are Special

All of us are special in Jesus' eyes—and that means *you,* all by yourself, just the way you are right now. We know from the Bible that Jesus has a special place in his heart for all kids. That's why he said:

> *"Let the little children come to me; do not stop them; for it is to such as these that the kingdom of God belongs."*
> *(Mark 10:14)*

Jesus truly understands how difficult things can be for a young person today. He knows about the dangers and disappointments, and he knows about the fun, silliness, and wonder, too. After all, Jesus was once a kid himself. Most importantly, Jesus does not want his beloved children to go through life feeling alone or scared. He wants to be there for each one of us, every step of the way, to help us and guide us and comfort us. Just as he wished it for Thomas à Kempis, Jesus wants us to know him, love him, and follow him, so that our life is joyful and fulfilling.

The Way Isn't Easy

Now, just like in your favorite movie or book, there are "good guys" and "bad guys" in the world. Some people out there just don't want you to follow Jesus. They are going to do their best to capture your attention and get you to follow *them* instead.

Think for a moment about your favorite computer game. Do you know how there are often weapons to be collected along the way to help fight against attackers? This book is like one of those special weapons. It will help protect you on your life journey from those who are determined to keep you from getting to the treasure—the *true* treasure: Jesus.

This book, based on the wonderful wisdom of Thomas à Kempis, is designed to help you learn how to survive this adventure called life by making the ultimate good guy—Jesus Christ— your true leader. It will also show you ways to make sure he stays in that position despite what the world may try to tell you. So follow along, step-by-step, on the most important and exciting journey you will ever make. This is learning for life!

Chapter One
Making Jesus the Leader

When you were younger, you probably played a game called "Follow the Leader." Maybe you played it on the playground at school, or with some friends in your neighborhood. Can you remember how this game was played? One person was chosen to be the leader. Everyone else had to copy whatever the leader did.

Copying people is an important way to learn. We start copying other people even from the time we're babies. Wiggle your tongue at an infant, and chances are she'll do the same right back! We may copy, or *imitate,* our parents, a big brother or sister, a teacher, our pastor, or a friend. Many times, we learn good behavior and habits by copying others. Sometimes, however, the people we choose to imitate may not always set the best example for us. When this happens, we end up acting in ways that can leave us feeling disappointed or even get us into trouble.

So How Do We Find Someone Good to Imitate?

God, our loving Father, has taken care of this problem for us. He loves us so much that he did something very special.

God sent his Son—in the form of Jesus Christ—to live on the earth among his people. God did this to teach us how we should live our lives and how we should treat one another. Jesus is the very best teacher and leader we can ever have. When we imitate the way Jesus lived and the way he treated those around him, we cannot be led astray! No one else can make that promise. Sometimes even people we know and trust can let us down, but Jesus will not. He promised he would be there for us forever. He said,

> *"And remember, I am with you always, to the end of the age."*   *(Matthew 28:20)*

Jesus is always there, no matter where we are, and he wants to be the leader in our lives. There is, however, one little catch.

It's really very simple: while Jesus wants to be our leader, he will never force us to follow him. He wants us to do that on our own, to follow him because we love him. That's worth saying again:

Jesus wants to be our leader, but he will never force us to follow him. He wants us to follow him on our own because we love him.

The Perfect Coach

Let's pretend for a moment that you play soccer. You have a terrific coach who has been known to win many soccer games. The coach will probably show your team exercises to make you strong and fast and give you plays to practice. But if no one follows

9

his instructions, you probably won't become better soccer players. Chances are you won't win many soccer games.

It's the same with Jesus, only Jesus isn't going to make you run ten laps around the field for not being a good follower. He is going to stand on the sidelines and love you anyway. He will wait for *you* to make him coach of a team that's guaranteed to win. That's because on Jesus' team you'll find happiness, peace, strength, and support—the winning combination for your journey. So let's stop running in circles trying to do it our way all the time and let's get on this winning team!

Jesus Is My Leader

The first thing we need to do is to make a promise to ourselves that Jesus is going to be our leader. But we can't just say these words once and forget about them. We have to mean them. We have to *keep* them. Perhaps you can write the words "Jesus is my leader" on a piece of paper and hang it in a place where you will see it during your day. Hang it by your bed, or maybe on the bathroom mirror. Every time you see your sign, you will remember that you have a leader and his name is Jesus. Every time other members of your family read your sign, they will remember that Jesus is their leader, too.

Next, we have to begin to get to know our leader. How do you get to know a new person at school? The best way, of course, is to go up and talk with that person. We need to do that with Jesus. It might make things a little easier if you can picture what Jesus looks like. You've probably seen lots of pictures of Jesus at church, in the Bible, and in other books. What does Jesus look like to *you?* Maybe your family can help you find a picture of Jesus that you like, and you can hang it next to your sign.

All Kinds of Ways to Talk

Now that your leader has a name and a face, talking with him should be a little easier. There are all kinds of ways to talk with Jesus. There are prayers like the "Our Father," grace at meals, or bedtime prayers that we know by heart. But did you also know that you can talk to Jesus the same way you talk to a friend or family member? He loves to hear about your day. Tell him about your fears and ask him your questions. Ask him for help with things that are difficult. Thank him for all the gifts he has given you: your body, your life, your friends, your family, your food, and your home. We don't always have to kneel by our bed or sit in a church to talk with Jesus. We can talk to him any time, any place. He's there to listen, day or night—he's never too busy or away on vacation.

Sometimes, however, *we* get busy—so busy, we forget to talk with God. It seems there is always someplace to go and something to do. You go to school, play sports, watch television, play with friends, read books, go to the movies, play video games, and do lots of other things. All these can be fun and even good for you, but we have to make sure that we don't get so busy that we forget all about our leader.

If you find this is beginning to happen, don't worry. You can just start again. Maybe it is as simple as moving your sign to another place to help you remember to keep your leader in your sight. Another good idea is to start and end your day with a little prayer to Jesus. You can wake up in the morning and offer your day to God, which just means that you "give" it to God—everything that happens to you, the good, the bad, and the in-between. At night you can simply thank him for the day you have just had.

Listening to Our Leader

One way of getting to know our leader is to talk with him. The other way is to learn to *listen* to him. The world is full of voices—loud, busy voices that are eager to tell us what we need and what will make us happy. The world tells us that to be really happy, we need to have lots of money and things. Many people grow up and spend their whole lives chasing money, success, power, and things. The more things they have, the more they want. Often, these people give themselves all the credit for what they have, instead of giving the credit to God. At the end, these people are still unhappy because they have not taken Jesus on the journey.

The things the world offers may be tempting, but they don't last long, and neither does the happiness these things bring. Even the most exciting toy or video game loses its appeal after a while. Only Jesus is lasting and true. That's why it's so important that we choose him as our leader and speak to him.

Jesus speaks to *us,* too, but we may need to listen extra hard to hear his voice over the loudness of the world. He speaks to us at church and through the Bible, of course. But he speaks to us in many other ways as well. He may speak to us in our thoughts. He may speak to us in the words of people around us. He may speak to us through books or songs.

How Will We Know His Voice?

How do we know when Jesus is speaking to us? We will know it is Jesus because his voice will bring us great peace. Also, when we make Jesus our leader, it becomes easier and easier to recognize his voice. He is the good shepherd who says:

> *"My sheep hear my voice. I know them, and they follow me."*   *(John 10:27)*

Making Jesus our leader does not mean we can't enjoy the things of the world. God created many beautiful things just for our pleasure. Heaven and earth were created for our use, and God wants us to enjoy them. He *wants* us to be happy. We must be careful, however, that we do not allow these things to replace Jesus as the leader in our lives. We need to keep things in balance, with God as the center. The Bible tells us that when we put God first, all our needs will be taken care of. Jesus said:

> *"Do not worry, saying, 'What will we eat?' or 'What will we drink?' or 'What will we wear?'…Your heavenly Father knows that you need all these things. But strive first for the kingdom of God and his righteousness; and all these things shall be given to you as well.*
>   *(Matthew 6:31–33)*

Our home, our food, our clothing, our bikes, and our games—everything we have is a gift and a blessing from God. All he asks is that we share these blessings with others.

Jesus Teaches Us to Love One Another

In the Old Testament, God gave his people a special set of rules called the *Ten Commandments*. These rules were meant to help his children live in peace and harmony, but the rules weren't always followed. That's why God sent his son, Jesus, to live among the people. Through his words and actions, Jesus gave the world the best example of how God wants us to live *our* lives. These lessons were not meant just for the people of the Bible long ago. They are important lessons meant for us today.

Think for a moment about any Bible story that has Jesus in it. Chances are, you will find him helping others. Jesus healed people's bodies, giving them the ability to see, to walk, and to live. He healed people's hearts, forgiving their sins. He showed us in one example after another how important it is to care for the sick, the poor, the children, and other people who are sometimes forgotten. Jesus was always thinking about others, even those who wanted to hurt him. He gave us this example of serving others so that we would do the same. Jesus taught us that besides loving God, loving each other was the most important thing of all. He said:

> *"I give you a new commandment, that you love one another. Just as I have loved you, you also should love one another."*   *(John 13:34)*

How Can We Love Other People?

If everyone followed Jesus' commandment, the world would be a better place. So how can *we* make a difference, and love one another the way Jesus wants us to? A good place to start is with our own families. We can help bring peace to our homes by respecting our parents and grandparents and by treating our brothers and sisters kindly. We need to ask ourselves some questions and to answer honestly: Do we listen to and obey our parents? Do we do our chores willingly and with a smile? Do we forgive our brothers and sisters when they have done something that hurts us? Do we ask for forgiveness when *we've* done something wrong?

We can love people outside of our families, too. Who else do we know that may be in need? Maybe it's a child on the playground with no one to play with. Maybe it's an elderly person alone at home or in the hospital who would really like a phone call or a visit. If we look around our world with the eyes of Jesus, we will see people who are sad, hungry, sick, lonely, or different—people who are hurting and people who could use a friend just like us!

But Thinking about Others Is Hard

Sometimes it's not that easy to think about others and what they need. It's much easier to think about what *we* need and what *we* want instead. The world tries to tell us that we have lots of wants and needs and that we deserve to get what we want, when we want it. What it doesn't tell us is that having to wait for things can be good for us. Even not getting things is okay, too.

Did you ever save your money for something really special? Do you remember how you felt when you finally had enough money to buy it? You probably enjoyed this item a great deal because you waited and worked for it. But sometimes when we

15

have to wait for something we think we really want, we may discover that we didn't really want it after all. Waiting helped us to learn this important lesson.

Learning to say "no" to ourselves, not getting our way all the time, sharing something we have with someone who needs it much more—these are all ways we begin to follow the example that Jesus showed us in the Bible.

J-O-Y!

Here is a fun and easy way to test yourself to see how you are doing in making Jesus your leader and serving others as he wants us to. If you put *Jesus* first, *others* second, and *yourself* third, the first letters of these three words—J (Jesus), O (others), and Y (yourself)—spell "JOY!" And joy is what you will feel because you are living the way God has planned. Every day, there are opportunities to live according to God's plan, to spread joy, and to *feel* joy!

Let's review what we've learned so far on the first part of our journey:

- Jesus is the best leader we can ever have.
- It's up to us to follow Jesus—he isn't going to make us do it.
- Talking to Jesus every day helps us to know him.
- Listening to Jesus is important, too.
- Jesus wants us to love one another. Find an opportunity to do that today and experience the joy!

Chapter Two
Becoming a Better Follower

Now that we've spent some time looking at our leader—Jesus—it's time we take a look at ourselves as his followers.

Did you ever stop and wonder why God put you on this earth? Was it just to eat food, go to school, play with friends, or ride a bicycle? God, of course, wants us to have fun and to be happy. He finds joy in *our* joy. But each of us was born to do something more. There is a reason that we are here. Each of us has a special purpose in life, one that is all our own, and our job is to find out what that purpose is. How do we do that? If you keep asking God about it in prayer, eventually he will help you discover your purpose in life.

So Many Ways to Love God!

Maybe your purpose is to be a priest or a sister. Maybe it is to be a married person with children. Your purpose may be to teach, to care for the sick, to write, to make music, or to discover cures for diseases. Whatever your purpose is, it should include loving and serving God and others. For example, if you want to grow up to be an athlete, be one who demonstrates good sportsmanship. If you want to be president, be one who truly cares

about the needs of the people. Maybe you would like to own a toy store or video game store. Be sure to treat others with honesty and respect.

When we find our purpose in life and begin to live it, we will find true peace and happiness. When we discover peace and happiness in our own lives, we can share it with the world around us. And that's how we can make a difference.

But I Don't Know What My Purpose Is Yet!

Don't worry. If you take God with you on your search, you will figure out why he put you here. Just remember that your life has meaning, and it has meaning *right now*. You don't have to wait to grow up! We can all begin today, right where we are, to bring the example of Jesus' love to those around us.

Choosing Goals

As a young person, you have your whole life ahead of you. It is good to have plans and dreams for your future. Maybe you are already thinking about what you want to be one day or where you want to live. But did you ever also think about what you want to do *after* this life?

Our most important goal for our future should be getting to heaven. Why? Because our true home is heaven. We are only pilgrims or travelers on this planet, visiting the earth for a short time. Heaven, on the other hand, lasts forever. Our experience of life on earth compared to our life one day in heaven is like comparing a single drop of rainwater to all the waters of the oceans—and their marvelous contents—put together. We can hardly imagine how vast and wonderful this place called heaven must be. And our way to heaven is to live the life we were given here and now, to live it fully as best as we can. We do that by following Jesus, our leader.

The "Be" Attitudes

On a grassy hillside on the shore of the Sea of Galilee, Jesus once gave a special talk to a large group of people. In this talk, Jesus listed some of the good qualities or *virtues* we should try to develop to be better followers. This talk became known as the *Sermon on the Mount* and the qualities Jesus listed became known as the *Beatitudes*. Another way to remember this word is to think of the qualities as the "*Be* attitudes"—ways we need to *be* to follow Jesus more closely.

In his talk, Jesus blessed people who rely on God and who are not overly attached to what they own. He blessed people who are sorry for their sins, and those who are humble and forgiving. Jesus also blessed people who stand up for things that are right, people who keep their hearts pure, and people who try to bring about peace. Lastly, Jesus blessed those who are made fun of or even punished for following his words and ways. Here is what he said:

> "*Blessed are the poor in spirit, for theirs is the kingdom of heaven.*
>
> "*Blessed are those who mourn, for they will be comforted.*
>
> "*Blessed are the meek, for they will inherit the earth.*

"Blessed are those who hunger and thirst for righteousness, for they will be filled.

"Blessed are the merciful, for they will receive mercy.

"Blessed are the pure in heart, for they will see God.

"Blessed are the peacemakers, for they will be called children of God.

"Blessed are those who are persecuted for righteousness' sake, for theirs is the kingdom of heaven.

"Blessed are you when people revile you and persecute you and utter all kinds of evil against you falsely on my account. Rejoice and be glad, for your reward is great in heaven."   (Matthew 5:3–12)

Putting the "Attitudes" into Action

Now that we understand that the Beatitudes are the way we need to "be" to follow Jesus more closely—let's talk about how we can make them a part of our own lives.

- **Be grateful.** It is important to realize that everything we have does not come from us, but from God. Therefore, we should thank him every day and remember to share our blessings with others.
- **Be understanding.** If we know someone who is sad or hurting, we can share his or her sorrow and help to comfort that person.
- **Be humble.** Look for opportunities to allow another person to go first, or to have the bigger or better part of

something. Also, a good follower of Jesus does not brag, show off, or disrespect parents or teachers.

- **Be forgiving.** Forgiveness goes two ways. We are called to forgive those who hurt us, and we are called to ask forgiveness when we hurt others.
- **Be pure.** We should stay away from people, things, or situations that will not help us to grow in holiness.
- **Be peaceful.** When we are peaceful, we can help bring that peace to others. One way is to be patient and kind and to help others to work out their differences with love.
- **Be proud of Jesus.** We should not be afraid to stand up for our faith and for what we believe, even when others think it isn't cool.

Living the Beatitudes is hard work, and sometimes we will fail. But Jesus will always help us to start over and try again.

Lead Us Not into Temptation

Jesus taught his apostles how to pray with very simple but special words known as "The Lord's Prayer" or, as it is often called, the "Our Father." You probably have been saying this prayer since you were a little child. There is a line in this prayer that says, "And lead us not into temptation." What does that mean? What exactly is a temptation and why does Jesus feel it is important enough to include in this prayer?

A *temptation* is something that tempts us, or pulls us, toward something that is usually not good for us. Everyone has temptations: parents and children, popes and presidents, athletes and

movie stars. Jesus himself was tempted many times in the Bible. Temptations are different for every person. We know when we are being tempted because deep inside we get an uneasy feeling.

How Are We Tempted?

There are lots of ways we may feel tempted. We may feel tempted to take something that doesn't belong to us or to tell a lie instead of the truth. We may feel tempted to watch television or play video games when we should be doing our homework instead. Maybe we feel tempted to ignore our parents when we are called, or to rush through a chore so we can get back to playing, or to not keep a promise that we made.

Our job is to know when we are being tempted, and to try and not give in to these feelings. Jesus can be a wonderful helper here. He knows exactly how temptation feels and he is ready to help us. We can ask Jesus every day to help us to be strong like he was with his temptations. And guess what? The more we resist our temptations, the stronger we become and the easier it gets to resist the next one. In the same way that exercising makes our bodies strong and healthy, working to resist temptations gives us strong "spiritual muscles."

What Happens When We Fail?

Since we are human, we all make mistakes. No one is perfect. When we give in to a temptation—and it will happen—it's not the end of the world. We can ask God's forgiveness and then start over again. We can pick ourselves up, just as Jesus did when he fell down three times while carrying his heavy cross.

The best way to start again is through the *Sacrament of Reconciliation,* also known as *Confession.* Not only do we receive God's forgiveness in this sacrament, but we also receive special graces to help us be stronger facing temptations the next time. God always thinks of everything!

Let's review what we've learned about being a better follower of Jesus:

- We were born for a reason and God can help us find our purpose.
- Jesus taught us how to be good followers with the Beatitudes.
- We need to practice these qualities in our own life.
- Temptations are a part of life, but following Jesus helps us to overcome them and be stronger the next time.

Chapter Three
Getting Closer to Jesus

As we get older, we grow in many ways. We become bigger and stronger and better at sports. Our brains grow, too, and we learn harder subjects in school. But we need to make sure we grow in faith as well. We shouldn't stop learning about God once we receive Holy Communion or have made our Confirmation. To keep Jesus as our true leader, we need to continue to learn and grow in our faith for the rest of our lives.

There are many things we can do now to help our faith grow along with our minds and bodies.

Get More Out of Mass

An excellent way to help our faith grow is to get more out of Mass. At Mass, we gather as a community of believers. First we are fed by God's word. Then we gather at the Lord's table and are fed the food of eternal life, his body and blood in the *Eucharist,* which is another name for Holy Communion.

The Mass is the most perfect way we can praise God. It has been celebrated in much the same way for thousands of years. Mass is so important, it takes place every day, even though most people go to church only on Sundays. All over the world, people celebrate the same Mass we do, but in different languages. That means that at every moment of the day or night, Mass is taking place somewhere in the world, and it will continue to take place until the end of time.

The readings and songs each Sunday have important messages for us. If we listen closely, we can hear God speaking through them, perhaps giving us some special advice or encouragement that we need to hear. Maybe he is answering your prayer questions or giving you directions about your special purpose. When *we* are listening closely, it allows other people to listen as well.

Of course, the most important part of Mass is Holy Communion. When the priest says the words of consecration, we need to show extra respect for God by kneeling quietly and asking him to help us be prepared to receive him in this special way.

Going to Mass is very important. Being a part of it is even more important. We do this with our prayers, our songs, and our good behavior. But there are other ways to participate in Mass. We can be an altar server, we can bring up the gifts of bread and wine with our family, or we can sing in a children's choir. All of these ways help our parish celebrate Mass more fully—and let *us* celebrate more fully, too!

Be Smart about Religion Classes

If you attend Catholic school, you have a regular class during the day called religion, where you learn about Jesus and his teachings. If you attend public school, you may take classes after school or at night in your parish where you learn the same things. These classes also help you prepare for sacraments like Reconciliation, Holy Communion, and Confirmation. Parents can also be good teachers of religion at home.

No matter how and where we receive our religious education, we should take it as seriously as we do any other subject— even more seriously. Listen closely, ask questions, and share your own thoughts and ideas. This is a subject you'll use for the rest of your life!

The Bible: The Greatest Story Book

Hopefully, you enjoy reading. Maybe you like adventures, or mysteries, or hero stories. Did you know the Bible is bursting with great stories? It has stories about giants, floods, battles, and miracles. A good children's Bible can present these stories in ways that you can understand and enjoy. Reading stories from the Bible helps us see the many ways that God loves his people and protects them. These stories also contain important truths and lessons for our lives.

Saints Alive!

Did you ever have someone special in your life die? That can really hurt, and you may miss that person a lot. But did you know that you can still talk to him or her in your prayers? You can ask that person to watch over you or help you when you need it.

Heaven is full of wonderful people who are our friends and helpers. When someone has been a very good example of following Jesus, the Church gives that person the title *saint*. Many saints have special days called *feast days* in which the Church remembers and celebrates their lives. But sainthood isn't just for a chosen few. *All* of us are called to be saints.

Saints can be men or women or even children. They can be priests, sisters, popes, workers, or stay-at-home moms. They can be rich or poor, healthy or sick. Some lived long ago and some not so long ago. They come from different countries all over the world, but all of the saints have one thing in common: they all loved God very much and can teach us important lessons about how to live.

Saints are ready to help us when we need it because they are very close to God. They can take our prayers before God and help us with the struggles we face. Many of them have suffered the same things we do, and this makes them want to help us all the more. Reading about the saints is a great way to get to know them, and there are many good books about saints for children. Some people talk in prayer to many saints, while others have just one or two favorites.

Were you named after a saint? This might be a person you want to learn more about. If you weren't named after a saint, there is still another opportunity at Confirmation, when you choose a Confirmation name. A Confirmation name should be the name of a saint who is important to you, a special friend that you want to be like. Read about these wonderful people now so you can find the right saint for you.

Jesus Is My Best Friend

We have come a long way on our journey. We have talked about making Jesus our leader, and we have learned some ways to make ourselves better followers. We are discovering on this

journey that the more we get to know Jesus, the more of a friend he becomes. Now let's take this one step further. Let's make Jesus our *best* friend.

A best friend is someone we can talk to who understands us. It is someone we enjoy spending time with, and someone we want to talk with often. A best friend accepts us as we are and forgives us when we make a mistake. Do you have a special friend in your neighborhood or at school that you like best of all? Jesus is an even better friend than that!

As our best friend, Jesus can be trusted with both the big things and the little things in our lives. He is interested in each one of us, and he wants us to come to him when we have to make decisions. When we face a difficult choice and take it to Jesus, we can be sure that he knows what is best for us, because Jesus knows everything.

A Friend for Good Times and Bad Times

Just like a best friend, Jesus shares our joys *and* our sorrows. Sometimes things don't always turn out the way we would like. Life can be wonderful, but it can also be very hard. Jesus understands this. He suffered many sorrows on earth, from the time he was born until the time he died. He was sad when three people he loved died—his earthly father, Joseph; his cousin John the Baptist; and his friend Lazarus. Jesus was made fun of and rejected by many people. He was arrested, spit upon, put in prison, tortured, and crucified. Therefore, Jesus really does understand when we suffer, especially when we suffer unfairly.

When we take our sorrows to Jesus, he gives us the strength to bear them. We can also offer up our suffering, give it to God, and join it with Jesus' suffering. This action brings great graces upon the world and helps others who are hurting, too. Sometimes remembering how other people hurt helps us not to feel so sorry for ourselves. Best of all, sadness or suffering can be a blessing at the same time. It can help us become stronger in our faith because it often makes us rely more on God and less on ourselves.

As Jesus becomes our best friend and an important part of our day, our love for him grows and grows. There's another way we can be even more closely joined with Jesus. Do you know how? It is through the sacraments, in which Jesus makes himself present in a very special way. The greatest sacrament of union with Jesus is Holy Communion, which we will discuss in the next and final chapter.

First, let's review what we've just talked about in following Jesus more closely:

- Our faith is something that should grow with the rest of us.
- We can help our faith grow by getting more out of Mass, paying attention in religion class, reading the Bible, and learning about the saints.
- Jesus wants to be more than our friend. He wants to be our *best* friend.

Chapter Four
Jesus Leads Us to Holy Communion

You have probably made your first Holy Communion by now, a very important step in your faith journey. Do you remember how excited you were to receive Jesus for the first time? You probably wore special clothes, and maybe you had a party afterward to celebrate. Your first Holy Communion was an important day because you were receiving Jesus in a new and special way.

Do you remember the second time you received Jesus? Maybe you wore your special clothes again, and it still felt new and exciting. What is Holy Communion like for you now? Do you still feel the same excitement you did the first few times? After we receive for a while, it is easy for us to forget what is happening during Holy Communion. It might begin to feel routine or even boring. When we forget the importance of the Eucharist, it becomes an empty sign for us instead of true food. We lose out on the graces this great sacrament offers us. It's like being given a sack of gold coins and putting it in our pocket and forgetting all about it.

JIMMY'S FIRST COMMUNION

THE PARTY !!

A SPECIAL MOMENT

HEAVENLY FRIENDS

The Most Important Sacrament

Holy Communion is the most important sacrament of all because Jesus is *truly present* to us there in a special way. Some Christian religions celebrate a communion meal with bread and wine as a sign or symbol of belonging together, or as a way of remembering the Last Supper. Catholics believe that this communion meal is much more than just a sign or a memorial. When Jesus said in the Bible, "This is my body....This is my blood," we understand the words exactly as he said them. Jesus also said:

> *"Very truly, I tell you, unless you eat the flesh of the Son of Man and drink his blood, you have no life in you. Those who eat my flesh and drink my blood have eternal life, and I will raise them up on the last day; for my flesh is true food and my blood is true drink. Those who eat my flesh and drink my blood abide in me, and I in them."*
>
> *(John 6:53–56)*

Therefore, at the moment of consecration, we believe that the bread and wine are no longer bread and wine, even though they still look and taste the same. The bread and wine have become Jesus—his body, blood, soul, and divinity. It is a special miracle that happens on Catholic altars all over the world, every day, ever since Jesus gave us this sacrament at the Last Supper. No one, not even grown-ups with lots of knowledge, not even the priest himself, can fully understand how this special union with Jesus happens. It is a deep mystery.

The good news is that we don't have to worry about knowing *how* bread and wine become body and blood. Jesus doesn't ask us to figure out his holy mysteries. He just asks us to live holy and faith-filled lives. Jesus wants us to accept and find joy in the wonders of our God! When we get to heaven one day, we will understand these mysteries and all the ways of God.

How Does Holy Communion Help Us?

Jesus gave us Holy Communion so that he can be with us in this close and special way for the rest of our life. The Eucharist has special graces, something like special powers, that strengthen us and help our faith and love for Jesus grow.

Receiving Jesus in the Eucharist helps us to be better followers. It helps us to resist those temptations we talked about earlier. It helps us to keep on the right path. The Eucharist refreshes us, heals us, and comforts us. In a way, it's like a super-powerful vitamin pill for our soul!

Preparing Ourselves to Be Ready to Meet Jesus in the Eucharist

Knowing that we are going to take part in the special miracle called Holy Communion should make us want to be prepared as best we can. Let's start with some things we can think about *before* we receive this sacrament.

All of us sin, old and young, no matter how hard we try not to. That's just a part of human nature. No one truly deserves the great gift of Holy Communion because of the poor choices we make from time to time. Jesus comes to us anyway in this sacrament, inviting us to be with him. Jesus is happy for us to come to his table. He promises to make up for whatever is lacking in us because with God, all things are possible.

Make an Examination of Conscience

Before we receive Holy Communion, we should prepare ourselves with a thoughtful *examination of conscience*. Do you remember learning about that when you prepared for your First Holy Communion? In an examination of conscience, we review our past thoughts, words, and actions to be more aware of what we've done wrong, so we can change, and what we've done right, so we can thank God. It is a good practice, both for children and adults. All we need to do is take a few moments before we receive Communion and ask Jesus to help us prepare our hearts for him. Then we should think about the past week and ask ourselves questions such as these:

- Have I been selfish or greedy?
- Did I talk badly about others?
- Have I been forgetting my prayers?
- Did I lose my temper?
- Did I tell a lie?
- Did I take something that didn't belong to me?
- Have I been wide awake and attentive for TV but distracted and restless in church?

Questions like these help us see things about ourselves that we need to work on to become better followers of Jesus. And remember, Jesus is always there to help us. All we have to do is ask. Sometimes, if something we've said or done is particularly heavy in our hearts, or if we haven't gone to Reconciliation in a while, we can ask God that our Communion give us the grace to go to Confession as soon as possible.

Receiving Holy Communion

Once we have examined our consciences, we are ready to approach Jesus in this special sacrament. It is very important that we always remember whom we are receiving in the Eucharist. It is Jesus himself! Therefore, we should receive the Eucharist with deep respect, awe, and humbleness.

Think about this. Before God became man in the form of Jesus Christ, the people had been given the word of God written on stone tablets. These tablets were contained safely in a gold chest called the *Ark of the Covenant*. This treasure was so holy and special to the people—even to the kings and prophets—that they treated it with great respect and honor. Now that we have Jesus—the word of God *made flesh*—shouldn't we honor this gift all the more?

Think also about how the Virgin Mary responded to the news from the angel Gabriel that she was to be the Mother of God. Our Blessed Mother received Jesus' body into her own with great love, respect, praise, honor, and happiness. We should try and follow her example. That's where our faith comes in. Ask Jesus to help you appreciate this great gift, and he will.

When Jesus died on the cross, he gave himself up as a sacrifice, or an offering, for our sins. He died so we can live with him one day in heaven. In receiving Holy Communion, we can imitate Jesus. We do not die on a cross, of course, but we can offer ourselves to God as a *living* sacrifice. We offer up to God all the sad and bad things that happen to us. We offer up all the good things that happen. We can also offer our very lives to God to use as *he* wishes. We can ask him to be our true leader and to help us be good followers by doing his work here on earth.

Receiving Holy Communion is also a good time to remember the needs of family and friends, those who are living and those who have died. We can offer these needs to Jesus in the Eucharist. Because there are so many blessings to gain from receiving Holy Communion, it is good to receive often, every day if we are able (that's one of the special blessings of our Catholic faith!) but certainly every Sunday.

After We Receive Holy Communion

After we receive Holy Communion, we should remain quiet and prayerful, enjoying the presence of Jesus within us. We are very blessed that God chooses to be as close to his people as he is in the Eucharist. With the graces we receive from this wonderful sacrament, we can change our lives and grow in holiness. We can become saints. We can stand up against the "bad" guys. *We can make a difference in this world.*

The very best prayer after Holy Communion is not words, but actions: to live in love and do God's will, just as Jesus did. That's why the priest ends Mass by saying, "Let us go in peace to love and serve the Lord."

To conclude, let us review what we have learned about Holy Communion, the closest way we can follow Jesus:

- In Holy Communion, Jesus is truly present.
- The Eucharist strengthens us to be better followers of Jesus and gives us many blessings.
- We should prepare ourselves carefully to receive Holy Communion.
- Loving God and serving others is the best prayer after Holy Communion.

Conclusion
A Final Word about Following Jesus

Do you remember our friend from the beginning of this book, Thomas à Kempis, who wrote *The Imitation of Christ?* Thomas was inspired to write that book because his heart was filled with love for Jesus and his teachings. Thomas wanted to follow Jesus as closely as he could, and he wanted the same for his community. So he used the wisdom Jesus taught in the Bible and showed his brothers practical ways that these lessons could come alive for them.

Thomas had no idea when he was writing his little book that it would one day become the most popular Christian writing after the Bible itself. *The Imitation of Christ* has been translated into more than ninety languages—more than any other book except the Bible—so that people from all over the world can read its valuable lessons. Today, millions of Christians, not just Catholics, have re-discovered their love for Jesus by reading Thomas's book. They have found it helpful in making the changes they need to in order to imitate Jesus more closely.

Thomas was simply following Jesus. When *we* follow Jesus, as we have learned, our lives will be happier and more peace-filled. But there's more—all the marvelous surprises God may have in store for us as his followers, not only for ourselves but for those around us. That's just one more great reason to follow Jesus!

Be happy and joyful! Jesus is our leader and we are invited to follow him in this life...and beyond.

"I am the light of the world. Whoever follows me will never walk in darkness but will have the light of life."
                                                        (John 8:12)

The Imitation of Christ for Children

Study Guide for Parents and Teachers

The timeless moral teachings of one of the greatest spiritual works ever written, *The Imitation of Christ* by Thomas à Kempis, is presented here for the first time in an interesting and easy-to-understand manner for young Catholic readers. Like the classic itself, **The Imitation of Christ** *for Children* is divided into four sections or chapters, taking the reader on a step-by-step journey into greater intimacy with Jesus Christ, culminating in the sacrament of the Eucharist.

Following are the highlights of each chapter, as well as suggested activities and discussion questions. These are geared for a wide range of ability and readiness in kids and can be used at home, in school, in religious education, and in Sunday school.

Chapter One

In the first chapter, the reader is invited to make Jesus Christ the leader in his or her life.

- Ask the child to create a simple sign or small poster, with the child selecting a visual representation of Jesus that he or she finds appealing.
- Discuss ways of talking to Jesus and to listening to what Jesus may be saying in return.

- Encourage the child to enter into dialogue with Jesus through various forms of prayerful conversation. Allow time and quiet for this.
- Encourage the child to begin developing the skills of listening for what Jesus may be saying in return. Allow time and quiet for this.

In this stage of the journey, the reader becomes aware that everything he or she has is a gift and a blessing from God, and that blessings are meant to be shared. The child is reminded of the other-centered life Jesus demonstrated on earth—healing, teaching, and forgiving—and is asked to look for opportunities in his or her life where that life-giving mentality can be applied. Jesus asks us to love one another. How can we show that?

- Discuss who needs my love this week. How can I show them that love?
- Have the child share his or her experiences in being Christ to another, and how that experience of sharing felt.
- Make a "J-O-Y" poster: *Jesus, Others, Yourself.* Find art and photos to represent these three categories. This creates a visual reminder that putting things in the appropriate priority will lead to ultimate happiness.

Chapter Two

The second chapter offers an opportunity for self-reflection on how I fare as a follower of Jesus. The child is asked to consider some important questions, perhaps for the very first time. The chapter also presents the Beatitudes as ways that enable people to follow Christ more closely.

- Have the child think about the following questions: Why am I here? What is my purpose in life? What do I want to be doing after this life? Allow time and quiet for this.
- Ask if anyone wants to share his or her thoughts about these questions or their answers.
- Review the Beatitudes with the child and what they mean.
- Help the child think of some people in the present or the past that embody particular Beatitudes.
- Ask the child to think of specific examples in his or her own experience to ensure that the concept is being understood.

Next, the subject of temptations is presented. It is important to stress that even though all people, from time to time, fail when faced with temptation, Jesus loves each one of us and is ready to forgive us every time.

- Ask the child to discuss (or to depict in visual form) some of the temptations he or she faces.

Chapter Three

This chapter presents practical ways that the young reader can mature in his or her own faith. These include understanding and participating more deeply in Mass and religious education, reading Holy Scripture, and learning about the saints.

- Attend a "teaching" Mass, one that walks the audience through the liturgy, taking time to explain each part. If one isn't available, try to arrange a teaching Mass through your local church or parochial school.
- Have the child read a Bible story and discuss it with the class or family.
- Help the child select a saint that he or she can study, share with others, and begin to know in a prayerful relationship.

A good start is the saint associated with the child's baptismal name.

As the reader grows in his or her relationship with Christ, Jesus will naturally become a bigger part of the child's life. The young reader is presented with the idea that Jesus is not only a friend, but a best friend, one who is always there, and one with whom the child can share anything.

- Discuss what a best friend is. Who are the child's best friends? Why?
- Discuss what Jesus might do as the child's best friend. Gently lead the child away from answers like "He'd give me a million dollars" with follow-up questions like "Name five things that are more important than a million dollars." If the child gives a tough response such as "He'd make my mother better" or "He'd bring my Grandpa back," gently lead the child away from that with statements like "Does your best friend really solve all your problems, or does he or she *stay* with you during your problems and help you be strong? How does Jesus stay with you? How does Jesus make you strong?" With prayer and reflection, you'll find just the right words for each child's own situation.

This concept fosters a feeling of genuine love toward Jesus, which makes the child more prepared to receive him in the most intimate way possible: the Eucharist, the subject of the fourth and final chapter.

Chapter Four

The book concludes with a chapter devoted to Holy Communion. In this section, the sacredness of the sacrament (focused on the real presence of Jesus) and its purpose in strengthening our faith are addressed for a better understanding of this special encounter with Christ. The chapter stresses preparation for this sacrament, including specific questions for a child-appropriate examination of conscience. These questions provide an excellent opportunity for further discussion. The chapter concludes with an explanation of what Holy Communion calls the recipient to do—to love God and serve others.

- Ask the child to think of a way he or she can love God and serve others this week. This can be in the form of a discussion or a craft.
- Ask what would be a way the child's family or class can love God and serve others as a group.

For Adults
from Elizabeth Ficocelli

The Fruits of Medjugorje
Stories of True and Lasting Conversion

This collection of first-person stories reveals the inspirational ways
that people have been deeply and permanently transformed
by these world-renowned visions of Mary.

*"This book will enhance the pouring forth upon the world the divine
grace flowing from Medjugorje and ultimately from heaven."*
—Bishop J. Faber MacDonald, Saint John,
New Brunswick, Canada

Paulist Press
$16.95
ISBN 0-8091-4388-7
Available at fine bookstores everywhere
or call 800-218-1903